CITIZENSHIP IN THE WORLD

BOY SCOUTS OF AMERICA
IRVING, TEXAS

**1986 Printing of the
1984 Revision**

Requirements

1. Explain how communications and transportation have changed relationships between countries. 7 8 & 9

2. Discuss the importance of international organizations with your counselor. Tell how the following organizations provide a means for countries to work together.
   a. United Nations
   b. World Court   11,12,13,14 & 15
   c. World Scout Association
   d. International Red Cross

3. Show on a world map countries that have different forms of government and ideologies from that of the United States. 17,18 & 19

4. Tell how the geography, natural resources, and climate of a country affect its economy. Tell how they may affect relations with other countries. England

5. Explain to your counselor what is meant by:
   a. International trade agreement
   b. Foreign exchange
   c. Balance of payments
   d. Tariffs
   e. Free trade
   How does world trade affect your community and state?

6. Show your counselor how the American dollar fluctuates in relationship to three or more major foreign currencies. Why are these currencies important to the United States?

Copyright 1984
Boy Scouts of America
Irving, Texas
ISBN 0-8395-3254-7
No. 3254   Printed in U.S.A.   35M1086

7. How does the U.S. State Department help us in foreign countries? What is meant by the following:
   a. International treaty
   b. Diplomatic exchange
   c. Ambassador
   d. Consul
   e. Cultural and educational exchange
8. Obtain the form to secure a passport. Fill it out and show it to your counselor.
9. Do ONE of the following:
   a. Attend a world jamboree.
   b. Take part in an international event in your area.
   c. Visit with a foreign exchange student and.discuss his or her country and customs.
   d. Take a year of foreign language in school.
   e. Write an embassy or consulate and secure material from it about its country and discuss the material with your counselor.

Contents

Introduction

Today thousands of people will call people in other countries by telephone, visit other countries as tourists, build products scheduled for export, and fly overseas to transact business.

Literally thousands of U.S. citizens find themselves "citizens of the world."

The rights and responsibilities of citizenship on a global basis, however, are less well defined than those established by national laws and constitutions. Independent nations recognize no authority higher than their own. The flow of trade and movement of people around the world are governed mainly by custom, international law, and treaties between countries.

All nations are dependent on other nations in some form—for products, for natural resources, for markets to sell their products, and for defense and other forms of assistance.

Rapid communications and world trade have made the world seem to shrink in size. There are more than 165 independent nations in the world, whose peoples speak 3,000 languages. However, many of the 4¾ billion people living in the world now find that they have direct interaction with each other. Citizenship in the world is a concept, based on the ideal of mutual understanding.

To comprehend this global community, you must be aware of the relationships among countries, the organizations that operate on an international level, and the mechanics of world trade.

Earning this merit badge will give you a foundation to better know the community in which all people live—the world.

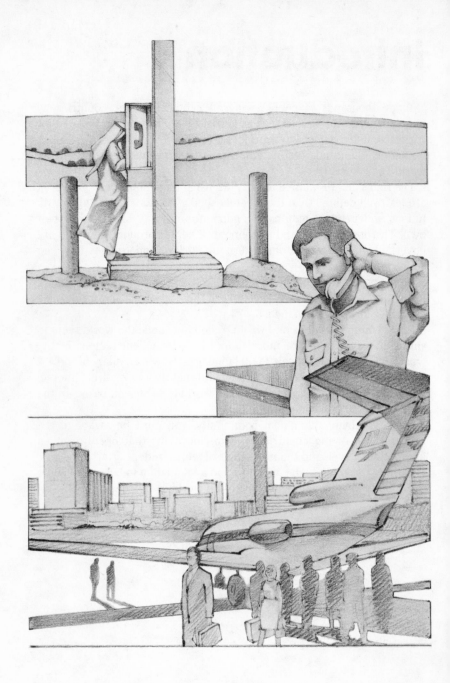

Communications and Transportation

Before the development of modern methods of communication and transportation the world seemed much larger. It took days and sometimes months for news to travel from one country to another.

During the War of 1812, for example, fighting continued for more than 6 months after the peace treaty had been signed before news that the war was over reached all of the forces. The most famous land engagement of the war, the Battle of New Orleans, was fought 15 days after the peace treaty had been signed. With modern methods of communication the war probably could have been avoided. The United States declared war on Great Britain for interfering with U.S. shipping. Two days before the declaration of war, however, the British government had decided to cease interfering with U.S. trade. Fighting had started before news of the decision reached the U.S.

Over the past 200 years, a variety of inventions have created a virtual revolution in communication and transportation that continues today. Most nations are now connected by complex communications and transportation networks, which provide for a massive exchange of information, of goods and services, and of people. Increasing dependence among nations has greatly changed international relationships and the way we view the world.

Communications

Modern communications systems transfer information quickly. Broadcast satellites transmit messages and images around the world in seconds. Worldwide broadcasting is made possible by the use of *synchronous satellites.* Three of these satellites, properly placed, can link any two parts of the world. They are called synchronous because their orbits are synchronized with the rotation of the earth; that is, they stay in the same relative position above the earth. These satellite systems are managed by the Communications Satellite Corporation (COMSAT) on behalf of the International Telecommunications Organization (INTELSAT), an agency that coordinates broadcasting between nations. The Soviet Union uses its own nonsynchronous satellite system.

With dozens of television channels available, a simple flick of the switch can bring to a viewer the Olympics in Yugoslavia, a flood in Japan, a speech in London, or a car race in France. Sights and sounds from throughout the world are readily accessible in most developed nations.

People in more than 80 countries can be reached by direct-dialing a telephone from the convenience of a home or office. For example, an American businessman can speak with an associate in Frankfurt, West Germany, by dialing the International Access Code (011), the country code for West Germany (49), the Frankfurt city code (611), then the local telephone number.

Communications satellites also link telegraph and telephone users in automobiles, ships, and airliners. Even the "hotline" between Washington and Moscow now is connected via satellites.

Other methods of communication such as photography, motion pictures, printing, computers, and video tapes have come into more widespread use through technological advances. The speed and ease of modern communications has brought more and better information to people throughout the world.

All of these forms of communication have helped to create closer international ties through their applications in business, entertainment, science, and the arts.

Transportation

With the development of modern methods of transportation, trade and travel between countries have greatly increased. This rise in the international movement of goods and people has made transportation one of the leading industries in the world.

Giant cargo ships, specially designed to carry specific products such as petroleum or grain, account for most international trade and are the cheapest means of transporting most goods. Pipelines, trucks, railroads, airlines, and inland waterways also carry international freight, especially in Europe, where countries are close together and actively trade with one another.

Refrigeration also has benefitted the transportation industry. Perishable goods now can be shipped great distances. Goods once available only locally are now available worldwide.

Sophisticated and effective transportation networks have had a profound influence on countries' economies. Nations now concentrate on making the goods they can produce most efficiently, such as rubber, wheat, machinery, or steel, for sale to other countries. Thus, more and better goods and services are produced through specialization. The United States is the world's largest trading nation. In addition to the manufactured goods it sells abroad, the U.S. also exports one-third of its agricultural production. Other industrialized nations also benefit from specialization and foreign trade, such as Japan with automobiles and cameras and West Germany with machinery. Foreign markets help boost a nation's economy, creating high levels of income and employment.

Jet airliners account for most international passenger traffic. Travelers can fly from New York to Paris in 4 hours, from London to Berlin in 1½ hours, and from Chicago to Tokyo in 14 hours. The speed and relatively low cost of international travel have made long journeys routine, whether for business or for pleasure. As a result, worldwide business connections have flourished, and the tourism industry has expanded. Tourism is one of the leading industries in many countries, such as Mexico, the Bahamas, and Spain.

Space travel is still in its formative stage. This form of future transportation is not yet economically feasible for moving large numbers of persons. However, several nations are cooperating with the United States in developing this technology. Many benefits already have been realized through the space program in the area of communications.

Worldwide transportation based primarily on engine-powered machines also has created worldwide problems, such as declining fuel reserves and environmental concerns. Many nations are working together to conserve natural resources, to develop alternate fuel resources, to improve the technology for tapping available fuel reserves, and to control pollution and other environmental hazards.

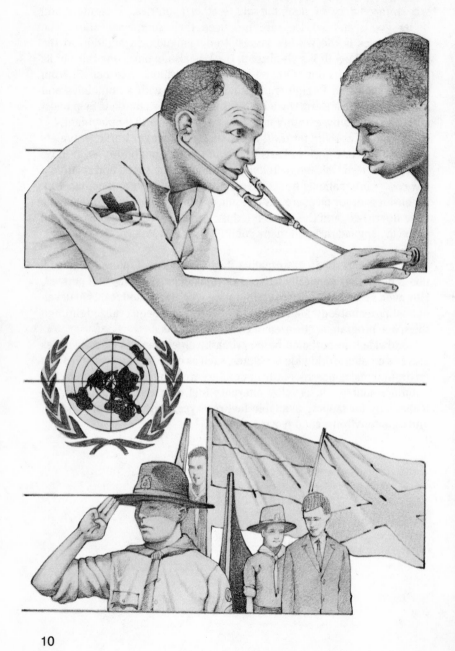

International Organizations

Many organizations operate in more than one country. These groups serve a variety of purposes and operate at different levels—between governments, businesses, communities, families, and other organizations.

United Nations

In June 1945, near the end of World War II, 50 nations that had opposed Japan, Germany, and Italy in the war formed the United Nations to maintain world peace. Since then, more than 100 other nations have joined the United Nations.

The United Nations headquarters is in New York City. Representatives of member countries meet there to achieve several goals: maintaining international peace and security; developing friendly relations among countries; and achieving international cooperation in economic, social, and cultural areas.

The United Nations has six main branches: the General Assembly, the Security Council, the Secretariat, the Economic and Social Council, the Trusteeship Council, and the International Court of Justice.

The General Assembly is the principal body of the United Nations, made up of all member countries, each with one vote. The assembly, sometimes called the "town meeting of the world," meets yearly and allows representatives of member countries to give speeches and to make recommendations and resolutions. The assembly has no power to enforce its policies; however, it does control the budget of the United Nations and decides how much money each member country should contribute.

The Security Council is composed of 15 member countries. Five of these countries—France, Great Britain, China, the United States, and the Soviet Union—are permanent members of the council. The other 10 members are elected by the General Assembly to serve 2-year terms.

Some of the functions of the Security Council are deciding what action the United Nations should take to settle disputes, including asking member countries to furnish military forces; approving all applications for membership in the United Nations; and selecting a candidate for the position of secretary-general, the top leadership position in the UN.

The Secretariat manages the day-to-day business of the United Nations and provides important services to UN agencies. The secretary-general is the head of the Secretariat. He advises governments, uses the influence of his office to help solve problems, and advises the Security Council. The secretary-general is nominated by the Security Council and elected by the General Assembly to serve a 5-year term. He may be reelected.

Outstanding international leaders have held this position. Trygve Lie of Norway, the first secretary-general, served from 1946 to 1953; Dag Hammarskjold of Sweden, from 1953 to 1961; U Thant of Burma, from 1961 to 1972; Kurt Waldheim of Austria, from 1972 to 1981; and Javier Perez de Cuellar of Peru, from 1982 to the present.

The Secretariat employs about 9,000 people. Half of them work at the UN headquarters in New York City and the others at the UN European office in Geneva, Switzerland.

The Economic and Social Council is composed of 54 member countries. The council acts as an advisory board, recommending ways to improve the health and welfare of the peoples in member countries.

The Trusteeship Council supervises territories that are not self-governing. The council, which meets once a year, is composed of representatives from the trustee countries and of representatives from the permanent members of the Security Council that do not govern trust territories.

The International Court of Justice, also known as the World Court, settles international disputes, interprets treaties, and advises the United Nations and its agencies on matters of international law. The World Court will be discussed more fully later in this chapter.

Other United Nations Agencies

The United Nations oversees several agencies that deal with the problems of world hunger, disease, poverty, education, and economic development.

The Food and Agricultural Organization (FAO) advises countries on such topics as soil conservation and the use of fertilizers. The FAO also grants fellowships to technicians, which enable them to study agricultural techniques in foreign countries.

The World Health Organization (WHO) advises countries on methods of maintaining public health and controlling the spread of diseases. This agency has had outstanding success over the past 30 years in eradicating many dreaded diseases in large sections of the world.

The International Labor Organization (ILO) works to promote social justice for workers. Among its projects are vocational training and educational programs for workers in developing countries. Delegates elected by member countries meet yearly and submit reports on the world union movement.

The United Nations International Children's Emergency Fund (UNICEF) helps children who need relief from hunger, sickness, and poverty. UNICEF is supported by contributions from governments and individuals, not by the UN budget. In the United States, many volunteers and civic organizations collect contributions for UNICEF on Halloween.

The World Bank, officially called the International Bank for Reconstruction and Development, lends money to help countries finance such projects as dams, irrigation systems, power plants, and railroads.

World Court

The International Court of Justice was established by the United Nations Charter and has its headquarters at The Hague, Netherlands. The Court is composed of 15 judges, each from a different nation. The judges are elected as individuals, not as representatives of their respective countries. The UN Security Council and the General Assembly each vote separately for the judges.

The judges settle international disputes. They interpret treaties, search for any violations of treaties, and determine the amount of damages. The court also gives advisory opinions to the United Nations and its agencies on matters of international law and interpretations of the UN Charter.

Only nations and certain international organizations may bring cases before the World Court. The nations must agree to submit to the court's decision before the court will hear the case.

World Scout Association

National Scouting organizations strive to promote the aims of Scouting through their international association—the World Organization of the Scout Movement. The World Organization is structured on three levels: the World Scout Conference, the World Scout Committee, and the World Scout Bureau.

The World Conference is the "general assembly" of Scouting, composed of national member associations representing more than 16 million Scouts and leaders in 150 countries and territories. One national association is recognized in each country. In countries with more than one Scout association, a federation is formed for coordination and recognition. The basis for recognition and membership includes adherence to the aims and principles of Scouting and an independent, nonpolitical, and voluntary operation. The World Scout Conference meets every 2 years.

The World Scout Committee is the executive body of the conference, representing it between biennial meetings. World Committee members are elected to 6-year terms at the World Conference, without regard to their nationalities. The committee has 12 members, with one-third retiring at each conference.

The World Scout Bureau is the secretariat that carries out the instructions of the World Conference and World Committee. Headquarters for the bureau are in Geneva, Switzerland, with regional offices in Yaba, Nigeria (African Region), Cairo, Egypt (Arab Region), Manila, Philippines (Asia-Pacific Region), San Jose, Costa Rica (Inter-American Region), and Geneva (European Region).

The World Bureau is administered by the secretary-general who is supported by a staff of technical resource personnel. The bureau staff helps national associations train their professionals and volunteers, establish sound fiscal policies and money-raising techniques, and improve community facilities and procedures. The staff also helps arrange world jamborees and serves as a liaison between the movement and other international organizations.

One of the major efforts being undertaken by the World Scout Organization is the extension of the universal "Good Turn" ideal in developing nations as a tool for community development.

International Red Cross

More than 120 countries have Red Cross societies organized to relieve human suffering. National societies maintain relations with other countries through the League of Red Cross Societies and the International Committee of the Red Cross, both with headquarters in Geneva, Switzerland. The League of Red Cross Societies represents member societies in international discussions and helps them develop programs and services. The International Committee of the Red Cross, made up of 25 Swiss citizens, works to protect war victims by serving as an intermediary between conflicting nations and to continually improve the Geneva Conventions, the agreement that provides for the humane treatment of prisoners of war. The Geneva, or Red Cross, Convention was first signed in 1864, and was later amended and improved. This treaty also provides for the treatment of the sick and wounded and for the protection of hospitals and ambulances bearing the Red Cross emblem.

Every 4 years the International Red Cross Conference meets in Geneva. Delegates from Red Cross societies and from governments that have signed the Geneva Conventions comprise the conference. They discuss the Geneva Conventions, cooperation between Red Cross societies and governments, and social welfare problems and concerns. The conference is the highest deliberative body of the Red Cross.

The name Red Cross comes from the organization's emblem, a red cross on a white field. The emblem is the reverse colors of the flag of Switzerland, where the organization was founded. In most Moslem countries the emblem is a red crescent on a white field, and the societies are known as Red Crescent societies. In Israel, the emblem is a red Star of David on a white field.

Most societies have developed comprehensive health and medical programs, and all societies provide humanitarian services, adhering to Red Cross principles. National societies provide emergency relief to victims of wars and disasters in other countries through their international affiliation.

Other Agencies

Many other international organizations work to improve the standard of living for people and to promote cooperation between countries.

For example, Save the Children is an agency that provides technical and financial assistance to children and their families in communities around the world. CARE, the Cooperative for American Relief Everywhere, supplies food, development assistance, and medical care and training in developing areas. The Salvation Army helps feed, clothe, and minister to the needy in 86 countries.

Religious organizations provide international benevolent programs through their social welfare and missionary agencies. Literally thousands of organizations throughout the world provide all forms of assistance to people and countries in need.

Forms of Government

All nations are ruled by one of three basic forms of government: rule by one person; rule by a few person; or rule by many persons, also known as *democracy*. All nations also employ one of three basic economic systems: capitalism, communism, and mixed economies.

Democracy

The United States is a federal republic governed by the principle of representative democracy. Under the federal system, certain powers are given to the national government and certain powers are given to the state governments. In a republic, qualified voters elect individuals to represent them and to enact laws on their behalf. Representatives are responsible to the people who elected them. Organization of the U.S. government was established by the supreme law of the land—the Constitution—in 1789.

Democratic governments are organized along two basic forms— presidential and parliamentary. Presidential democracies like the U.S. provide for three branches of government: legislative, executive, and judicial. Members of the legislative branch and the top officials of the executive branch—the president and vice-president—are elected to fixed terms of office. Parliamentary governments combine the legislative and executive branches. The head of government is known as the prime minister, who is a member of the political party in power in the legislature, or parliament. A prime minister does not serve for a fixed term, but rather for as long as he or she has the confidence of parliament. Confidence is determined by votes on key issues and by national elections when another political party may gain the majority vote in parliament.

Examples of other countries with presidential democracies are Mexico, France, and Brazil. Examples of countries with parliamentary democracies are Great Britain, Canada, and Denmark.

Many countries that were once governed by *absolute monarchs,* rulers with unlimited powers, have adopted democratic principles and have given their citizens a much greater voice in the government. These countries, while retaining the monarch as a ceremonial head of state, are now called *constitutional monarchies*. Some nations that have this form of democratic government are Great Britain, Japan, and the Scandinavian countries.

In truly democratic societies, citizens are guaranteed the rights to make their governments responsive to their wishes. In addition to the right to vote, U.S. citizens are guaranteed the freedom of speech, of assembly, of religion, and of seeking public office. Citizens may demand that a public official be removed from office. Citizens also may organize political parties and special-interest groups to promote certain programs and ideas. Public opinion is an important factor in representative government. The protection of individual rights and indirect self-government are the two chief features of the U.S. political system.

Capitalism

The economic system used in the U.S. is capitalism, also known as *private enterprise* or *free enterprise*. In a capitalistic system, almost all goods and services are owned and produced by individuals and private companies, with some government regulation. Since the private sector determines the goods and services that will be produced and how much they will cost, competition among producers is a chief feature of capitalism.

Examples of other nations with economies based on the private enterprise system are Canada, West Germany, and Japan.

Communism

In contrast to the democratic, capitalistic nations are the communist nations. Communism is both an economic system and a political system. In these countries, political power lies in the hands of relatively few people. Opposition to the government is severely limited and there are few individual rights. Only members of the Communist party have any voice in the government, which establishes educational, health, housing, social, and cultural programs. In the communistic economic system, the government directs the production of goods and services and owns almost all industries. Central planning is the chief feature of communism.

China and the Soviet Union are the two largest communist nations. Other communist nations are in Southeast Asia and Eastern Europe. Cuba is the only communist nation in the Western Hemisphere. Almost one-third of the people on earth live in communist countries.

Tension and conflicts arise between democratic nations and communist nations because their ways of life are based on different *ideologies.* An ideology is the body of ideas that social, political, and economic systems are based on.

The democratic system is based on individual liberties and the free exchange of ideas. Most democratic nations are termed *pluralistic* because the government, private companies, and individuals all share in controlling the country's activities. Political power is vested in the people.

The communistic system is based on the needs of the state. The aim of communism is the equal distribution of goods and wealth. The government controls almost all the country's activities. Political power is vested in a single, authoritarian political party.

Dictatorship

Many developing nations have tried to establish governments based on democratic principles, but because of economic and political problems these nations often are ruled by a single person or a small group. This type of government, as well as communistic government, is often referred to as a *dictatorship.* The leaders of many developing nations are military officers who came to power with the backing of their country's armed forces. This type of military government is often called a *junta.*

Examples of countries ruled by a military dictatorship are Libya, Ethiopia, Afghanistan, and Chile. Examples of countries ruled by a civilian dictatorship are the Philippines, South Korea, Haiti, and Central African Republic. Saudi Arabia is one of the few countries in the world still ruled by an absolute monarch.

Many communist countries and developing countries ruled by dictatorship refer to themselves as "republics" or "people's democracies." However, the people in these countries have little or no voice in their government.

Mixed Economics

Most developing nations operate with a mixed economy—the private sector produces goods and services and the government owns and operates basic industries, such as railroads, mines, and factories.

Many democratic nations also operate with a mixed economy. The governments of Great Britain and Sweden, for example, own and operate many of their countries' basic industries. Citizens in these countries pay very high taxes and receive extensive social welfare benefits in return. This type of economy often is called *democratic socialism.*

Geography and Resources

A country's economic and political position in the world is determined by its location, terrain, natural resources, climate, population, and industries. All of these factors define which goods a country produces and its standard of living. Geography also affects transportation systems and trade within a country and commerce with other countries.

For example, Australia is an isolated nation-continent located thousands of miles from its trading partners, with abundant space and natural resources and relatively few people. Therefore, Australia produces agricultural and mining products for export and imports manufactured goods. In contrast, Switzerland is a small, densely populated country with few natural resources located amidst its European trading partners. Therefore, Switzerland produces manufactured goods for export and imports raw materials and agricultural products. Both nations enjoy a high standard of living. They have developed their most efficient industries and are active in international trade.

Australia has built extensive rail, air, and shipping lines to link its scattered population centers, and relies on giant cargo ships to transport its beef, wool, and minerals to foreign markets. Switzerland also has an effective transportation system, in spite of the country's mountainous terrain, and relies on a variety of transportation methods to send its electronic equipment, machinery, and watches to foreign markets.

Less developed countries often face problems because of their geography. For example, Paraguay is a small, landlocked country in South America with a small population and poor transportation systems. Even though the country has good soil, mineral deposits, and a temperate climate, most of its people live by subsistence farming. The country also has suffered from political instability.

Zaire, in central Africa, has a large population, ports, and is rich in minerals. Most of the people in this developing nation also live by subsistence farming. However, Zaire is one of the leading exporters of copper, and it also supplies its trading partners in Europe, North America, and Japan with industrial diamonds, coffee, and cobalt. The country imports oil, manufactured goods, food, and textiles. The development potential for Zaire is good because of its mineral wealth.

The wealth and economic development of a nation often depends on its natural resources. The U.S., the Soviet Union, and West Germany are examples of developed nations rich in a variety of natural resources. Many countries with abundant natural resources and the technology to use them have developed great national wealth, such as South Africa with diamonds, Saudi Arabia with oil, and Canada with timber products. Most of the poor nations of the world have few natural resources.

Economic growth in developing countries is difficult because of high birth rates, disease, illiteracy, and the lack of modern equipment. About three-fourths of the world's population lives in developing countries. Many of the countries rely on the rich, industrialized nations to provide them with financial aid and technological assistance. Developing nations, also known as the *Third World,* comprise a majority of votes in the United Nations. Third World countries increasingly are demanding a redistribution of the world's wealth to help solve their economic problems. *First World* countries are the industrialized, non-Communist nations. *Second World* countries are the Soviet Union, the communist countries of Eastern Europe, and Cuba.

Mineral natural resources—fuel and raw materials—are vital to transportation and the manufacture of finished goods. A nation lacking these natural resources must import them. Even though the U.S. has petroleum reserves, it must import large amounts of petroleum to satisfy its industrial and transportation needs.

Many developing nations have primarily agricultural economies. However, these countries often must import additional food because their people farm with inefficient agricultural methods. Japan boasts an efficient agricultural system, but the mountainous island nation must import nearly one-third of its food to support its large population.

Nations rely on one another to buy and sell natural resources to satisfy their economic needs.

Climate also affects the agricultural and transportation systems of a country. Precipitation and temperature extremes dictate which crops can be grown and may hamper efficient transportation.

For example, many less developed nations are located in the tropical areas of the world. Rice, fruits, and vegetables can be grown in these regions, but heavy forest growth and rains impede the construction and maintenance of roads. People in these countries rely mainly on water transport. Poor transportation and low incomes often result in people having inadequate diets. Malnutrition is a serious problem in many developing nations.

In the U.S., diverse climates and soils allow farmers to grow a variety of crops. Agricultural products are a major part of the U.S. economy. Farms and ranches supply all of the nation's basic food needs as well as a large surplus for sale abroad. Efficient transportation systems ensure that all of these products are available nationwide.

Cold temperatures for most of the year also have an adverse effect on a country's economy. The frigid zones of the earth are sparsely populated. Most productive societies lie in the temperate zones, where the seasons and various weather conditions encourage production.

Most industrialized nations, including the U.S., have implemented extensive foreign aid programs to assist developing countries. These programs consist of financial assistance, technological development, health care, education, and other areas vital to a country's growth and well being.

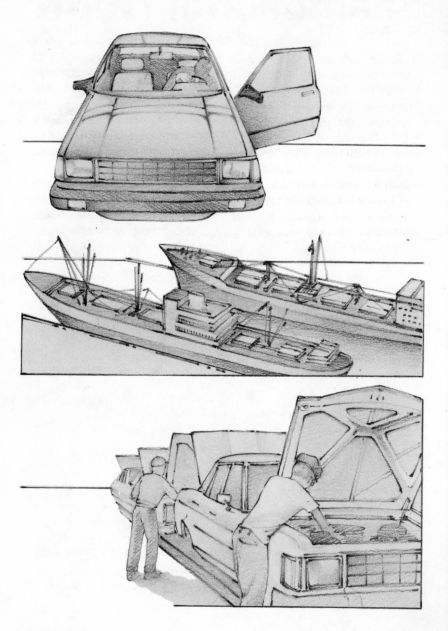

International Trade

The exchange of goods and services among countries is known as international trade, world trade, or foreign trade. It is a diverse process that includes transactions of raw materials, finished goods, travel, and gold. The growth of international trade has allowed countries to specialize in producing those goods and services they are best equipped to make. This specialization has resulted in more and cheaper goods and services, especially in industrialized nations. A country benefits by concentrating on producing the goods it can make most efficiently and by buying goods other countries make most efficiently.

Most international trade is carried out among developed, industrialized nations, especially the U.S., Canada, France, Belgium, the Netherlands, Sweden, West Germany, Japan, Italy, and Great Britain. Private companies and individuals handle most international trade; governments handle a small portion. However, in communist countries government agencies are responsible for all international trade.

All nations establish trade policies. These policies provide for the mutual exchange of goods between countries, and often place barriers against the importing of certain goods.

International Trade Agreement

To promote and develop trade, countries often sign treaties called *international trade agreements.* These agreements give special treatment to the participating countries—trade barriers are eased and countries often agree to buy specific products from each other.

The most important international trade agreement is the General Agreement on Tariffs and Trade (GATT). About 90 countries have signed GATT agreements, which mainly deal with reducing trade barriers. Members of the GATT are called *contracting parties.* Representatives of the contracting parties meet to establish rules to reduce tariffs and other trade barriers and to review complaints concerning violations of the agreement. Contracting parties basically agree to follow a code of commercial policy aimed at promoting world trade. International trade barriers to thousands of products have been reduced through the efforts of GATT conferences.

Foreign Exchange

Because different countries have different monetary systems, importers must pay for a foreign product with that country's currency. Domestic money must be exchanged for foreign money. This purchase of foreign currency is carried out in a foreign exchange market, where different currencies are bought and sold. For example, a U.S. company that imports steel from Belgium exchanges U.S. dollars for Belgian francs to pay for the material. The price of francs in dollars is known as the *foreign exchange rate.*

Balance of Payments

A financial record of a country's transactions with other countries is called a *balance of payments.* This record measures the amount of money earned through exports and the amount of money paid for imports.

Profits from exports such as business investments in other countries, the sale of agricultural commodities and manufactured goods, and money spent by foreign tourists are considered positive balances.

Imported commodities and manufactured goods, citizens traveling abroad, and foreign aid or loans contribute to negative balances.

If more goods and services are bought from foreign countries than are sold to them, a country has a deficit in its balance of payments. If more goods and services are sold to foreign countries than are bought from them, a country has a positive balance of payments.

A country's balance of payments affects the value of its exchange rate. A positive balance of payments will cause the exchange rate to rise; a negative balance of payments will cause the exchange rate to drop.

For example, the U.S. exports $400 million more than it imports from Italy; therefore, the U.S. has a positive balance of payments and Italy has a negative balance of payments. The U.S. imports $2 billion more than it exports to Japan; therefore, the U.S. has a negative balance of payments and Japan has a positive balance of payments.

Tariffs

Taxes imposed on imported goods by governments are known as tariffs. Tariffs are used for two reasons: to protect domestic industries and to raise revenue for the government.

Adding the expense of taxes to imported goods increases their price, encouraging consumers to buy domestic goods. This type of import tax is known as a *protective tariff.* Less important are *revenue tariffs,* taxes placed on imported goods to generate income for a government. Revenue tariffs often serve as protective tariffs if they increase the price of imported goods so as to make them less competitive than domestic goods.

Tariffs are used to protect developing industries, to protect industries vital to a nation's defense, to protect jobs, and to prevent foreign competition from closing established businesses. Tariffs usually are imposed through the urging of special interest groups, organizations of businesses or workers, or both, that want protection from foreign competition for their industry.

Tariffs are collected in various ways. These import taxes, or duties, can be applied to the weight or volume of a product or to the market value of a product. Compound duties are a combination of these two methods. Most raw materials are taxed according to their weight or volume. Most manufactured materials are taxed according to their market value.

Other trade barriers used by governments are *import quotas,* which limit the number of products allowed into a country, and *import licensing,* which requires an importer to get a government permit before bringing goods into a country.

For more than 30 years, non-Communist industrial nations have worked to reduce tariffs and thus increase trade. Industrialized nations seek to reduce import barriers to expand the markets for their products. For example, several nations in Western Europe have formed the European Economic Community, also known as the Common Market, to remove the trade barriers among member nations. Members trade freely with one another, but the EEC maintains tariffs on goods from outside its membership.

Reciprocal trade agreements provide a means for two countries to establish mutually beneficial tariff rates. These agreements often include a most-favored-nation clause, which requires countries to apply their lowest tariff rate on all products exchanged between them.

Developing countries maintain high tariffs to promote domestic economic development. Many of these countries, however, have organized trade associations to increase the flow of goods among themselves.

Communist countries usually are not important participants in international trade, even though they have removed some trade barriers from one another's products. The Soviet Union and China have shown an interest recently in increasing their international trade connections.

Economic and political goals are reflected in a country's trade policy. As these goals change, trade policy changes. For example, until the Great Depression in the 1930s the United States followed a protectionist policy with high tariff rates. Since then, the government has gradually reversed this policy. Today, the U.S. generally advocates a policy of free trade.

Free Trade

Trading between countries without imposing any restrictive barriers is known as free trade. This concept is based on the principle of comparative advantage. Simply stated, this principle asserts that producers will specialize in making goods as cheaply as possible with available resources. Goods that can be made cheaper elsewhere, such as in other countries, can be bought from those producers. Through specialization and active international trade, worldwide production increases and consumers are supplied with a wide variety of competitively priced goods.

Nearly 4.8 million American workers owe their jobs to the export of manufactured goods. Industrial products such as aircraft, machine tools, and trucks are widely exported from the U.S. More than 35 percent of the annual agricultural production in the U.S. is sold abroad, including such crops as cotton, soybeans, corn, tobacco, and wheat. The three largest exporters in the U.S. are General Electric, Boeing, and Caterpillar Tractor.

Imports also are important to the U.S. economy. The U.S. imports almost 40 percent of the world's copper, iron ore, nickel, oil, coffee, and tea. By 1980, imports accounted for nearly $300 billion worth of goods being received each year. Products made in Japan, Sweden, West Germany, and many other countries are available in most retail stores. International products—from toys to automobiles—have become an everyday part of American life.

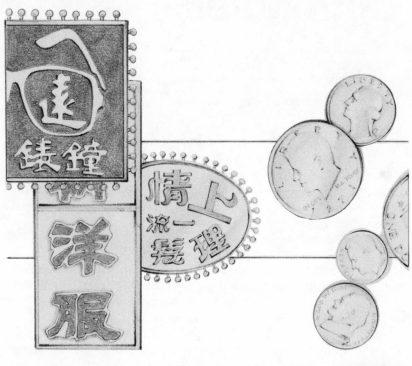

Currencies

Each country has its own system of money, or currency, that carries a certain value as a medium of exchange. Currencies are not interchangeable. For example, U.S. dollars are not the same as Canadian dollars, Mexican pesos, or Swiss francs. A method of exchanging currencies is necessary to pay for foreign goods.

The foreign exchange rate is the market price for a country's currency. The rate determines how much foreign currency an importer or exporter can expect in exchange for domestic currency. For example, a U.S. car dealer who buys Volkswagens from West Germany may have to pay for them in German marks. The car dealer, through a bank or special brokerage firm, would exchange dollars for marks to pay for the cars.

The cost relationship of foreign currencies to the U.S. dollar can be expressed in units per dollar. The car dealer, for example, could have purchased marks for 40 cents each, or 2½ marks for each dollar. A Volkswagen with a price of 25,000 marks would therefore cost the dealer $10,000. If the exchange rate for the mark dropped to 39 cents, the car dealer's cost for the car would drop to $9,750.

Major trading nations allow the exchange rate of their currencies to fluctuate according to demand for the currency. This is called a *floating exchange rate,* and has been used since the early 1970s. Exchange rates may change on a daily basis. The exchange rate on any given day is called the *spot rate.* Financial institutions that serve as international exchange markets also buy and sell contracts for the future delivery of currencies. This exchange rate is known as the *forward rate.* Newspapers and financial publications such as *The Wall Street Journal* publish daily listings of the spot rates and the forward rates of major currencies.

Exchange rates are important to trading companies and to travelers because they indicate how much foreign goods or services cost in terms of their own currency. Traders and travelers can then compare the cost of foreign goods and services with the cost of domestic goods and services.

As with all national currencies, the exchange rate of the American dollar is influenced by its demand on international exchange markets as well as by economic conditions within the U.S. The greatest demand for U.S. dollars comes from America's major trading partners, such as Japan, West Germany, Great Britain, France, Canada, and Mexico. On one day in 1983,the exchange rates for the U.S. dollar were $1.50 for the British pound, 80 cents for the Canadian dollar, 39 cents for the West German mark, 12 cents for the French franc, .006 cents for the Mexican peso, and .004 cents for the Japanese yen. The major money markets that determine the value of the U.S. dollar are in London, Toronto, Paris, Tokyo, Zurich, and Frankfurt.

Countries will not allow their exchange rates to fall too far. All countries keep a special stock of foreign currencies known as the *international reserve.* When a currency decreases too much, a country will buy some of its own currency back with its international reserves to stabilize the exchange rate.

Since the United States is the leading trading nation in the world, most countries keep their international reserves in U.S. dollars, and most countries will accept U.S. dollars as payment. The dollar often functions as an international monetary unit. The exchange rate of the dollar, therefore, is not only important to the United States but to those countries that fund their international reserves with dollars.

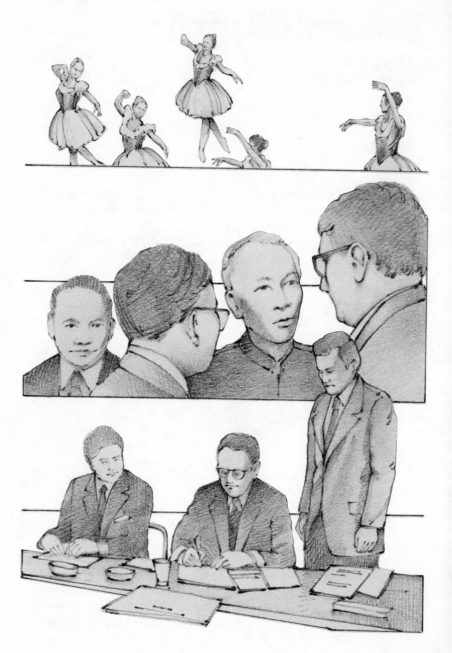

34

International Relations

The U.S. Department of State is responsible for all official relationships with the governments of other countries. The chief officer of the State Department is the secretary of state, who is appointed by the President and confirmed by the Senate. His main functions are to advise the President on foreign relations and to carry out U.S. foreign policy. The secretary of state also must develop plans to deal with international problems.

Foreign policy is the official, planned actions the U.S. takes in dealing with other governments. Foreign policy is developed by the State Department and approved by the President.

The State Department also negotiates treaties and agreements with other countries and represents the U.S. before the United Nations and other international organizations. The department also is the official liaison with foreign embassies in Washington, D.C.

Representing the U.S. in other countries are members of the Foreign Service, professional employees of the State Department. Foreign Service officers, through their dealings with officials of other governments, report to the State Department on foreign affairs that affect the U.S. These reports are a primary basis of U.S. foreign policy. Other duties of the Foreign Service include issuing passports, granting visas to tourists and immigrants coming to the U.S., and protecting the interests of U.S. citizens and businesses in foreign countries.

International Treaty

A formal agreement between two or more nations concerning economic or political matters is known as a treaty. Governments signing a treaty promise to fulfill certain obligations. In the U.S., a treaty must be approved, or ratified, by the Senate.

Treaties signed by two nations are known as *bilateral* agreements; treaties signed by several nations are known as *multilateral* agreements.

Nations enter into treaties for a variety of purposes. Commercial treaties establish trading rules between countries, such as goods to be exchanged and tariff rates. Political treaties usually establish provisions for mutual defense among countries. The North Atlantic Treaty Organization is an example of such an alliance. The U.S., Canada, and 13 European countries have signed this mutual-defense pact. Some political treaties establish closer cooperation among countries. For example, the Helsinki Agreement, signed in 1975, was formulated to reduce international tensions. The treaty was signed by the U.S., Canada, and most European nations, and provides for greater cultural and economic exchanges between communist and non-Communist nations. The agreement also deals with human rights issues.

Other treaties deal with the extradition, or return, of criminals and fugitives; copyright and patent protection; and arms limitations.

Diplomatic Exchange

Nations establish official relations by exchanging accreditated representatives known as *diplomats*. These representatives protect and promote their country's economic and political interests in the host country. Diplomats cultivate contacts with officials and important citizens of the host country and gather information of interest to their governments.

Since diplomats are the official spokespersons of their governments, they remain under the authority of their governments and enjoy a privilege known as *diplomatic immunity.* Established by international law, this principle states that diplomats are protected from arrest, from taxation by the host country, and from search and seizure of their belongings and papers.

Diplomatic headquarters are are called embassies or legations, depending on the rank of the diplomat in charge. Ambassadors direct embassies; ministers direct legations. All diplomats report to their country's foreign office, known in the U.S. as the Department of State.

Ambassador

The highest diplomatic rank is that of *ambassador extraordinary and plenipotentiary.* Ambassadors are in charge of their country's diplomatic mission in a foreign capital and are the official communications channel between the two governments. An ambassador serves as the personal representative of his or her country's head of state.

In the U.S., ambassadors are appointed by the President and approved, or confirmed, by the Senate. Most U.S. ambassadors come from the ranks of the Foreign Service. All countries with which the U.S. has formal diplomatic relations are sent ambassadors, who coordinate all U.S. activities in those countries.

In addition to managing the embassy staff, an ambassador handles economic, political, and cultural negotiations with the top officials of the host country.

Diplomatic ranks below an ambassador are envoy extraordinary and minister plenipotentiary, minister resident, minister-counselor, counselor of embassy, secretary of embassy, and attaché.

Consul

Governments also appoint representatives to look after their commercial interests in foreign countries. These representatives are known as *consuls.* A consul is in charge of a consulate, which functions much the same as an embassy but is located in a major city rather than the capital. Depending on the size of a country and the complexity of its trade, consulates may be located in most major population centers. Consuls are concerned primarily with promoting their country's business interests.

As with the diplomatic service, the consular service is divided into ranks. The highest consular rank is consul-general, followed by consul and commercial agent. In the U.S., the Foreign Service is made up of the diplomatic and consular services.

Consuls must be officially recognized by their host country, and their duties often are spelled out by commercial treaty. The difference between a consul and a commercial agent is that a commercial agent does not have the official recognition of the host country. All consuls in a given district report to a consul-general.

Since U.S. consuls are official representatives of the government, they also assist U.S. citizens by issuing birth, death, and marriage certificates and by helping those who have been arrested or robbed.

Consulates are located in most large cities in the U.S., such as New York, Chicago, Los Angeles, San Francisco, New Orleans, and Houston.

Cultural and Educational Exchange

To promote international understanding, nations often agree to exchange artists, students, and scholars to allow them to perform, to study, and to conduct research.

An example of a cultural exchange would be a Russian ballet troupe traveling to the U.S. and an American symphony traveling to the Soviet

Union. Cultural exchanges increase awareness of other peoples' traditions in art, literature, and science.

Educational exchanges give students the opportunity for foreign travel and learning experiences. Programs established by such groups as American Field Service, Youth for Understanding, Experiment in International Living, and Rotary International select students to visit and study in foreign countries. More than half a million students have taken advantage of these programs over the past 10 years. Educational exchanges give students a first-hand experience of everyday life in another country.

Passports

A valid passport is necessary for entering most foreign countries and for reentering the United States. A passport is a government document issued to citizens for travel abroad. It is basically an identification certificate that entitles the bearer to the protection of his own country and to the protection of the country visited.

Some countries require travelers to have a visa, which is a special endorsement that allows a person to enter or travel through a country. A visa signifies that the proper official has examined a passport.

Passports are issued by the U.S. Department of State. Applications are available at post offices. To obtain a passport, a person must submit proof of U.S. citizenship (a birth certificate or naturalization papers), and furnish two identical recent photographs (2 inches square on a white background). A person also must provide proof of identity, such as a driver's license or a witness who will testify to the individual's identity. The issuing agent will then check and verify these documents, witness the applicant's signature, collect the passport fee, and submit the application to the Passport Office. Passports are valid for 5 years for applicants 17 and under, and valid for 10 years for adults.

To determine current visa requirements, write to the U.S. Department of State, Bureau of Consular Affairs, Passport Services, 1425 K Street NW., Washington, DC 20524, and request the pamphlet titled "Visa Requirements of Foreign Governments."

U.S. citizens do not need passports to travel to Canada, Mexico, Bermuda, and most countries in the West Indies

International Events

Learning about the customs and traditions of other countries is important in an increasingly interdependent world. A variety of opportunities are available for experiencing different cultures.

A world jamboree is a fascinating event. Scouts from all parts of the world gather every 4 years in a different country to meet other Scouts and to make international friendships. At jamborees, Scouts camp together, compete in Scout skills, sample each other's food, and learn words and phrases in other languages. The friendships made at these gatherings overcome barriers of language and differences in custom, race, and religion. Participation in a world jamboree is a Scouting highlight.

Other international events are celebrated throughout the U.S. Heritage parades, folk festivals, cooking schools, and museum exhibits promote understanding of different cultures. Almost all communities have activities with an international flavor that are interesting and enjoyable.

Another way to learn about other countries is to visit with a foreign exchange student. Many students from other countries come to the U.S. each year to study American culture. These students can offer interesting insights into the way they live at home, and to the similarities and differences between their country and the U.S.

Knowing a foreign language is a valuable skill, and one that is helpful in understanding another country and its people. Speaking another language not only increases the ability to communicate, but the ability to comprehend different ways of thinking and behaving.

Good sources of information about other countries are their representatives living in the U.S.—the diplomats and consuls. Most foreign embassies are located in Washington, D.C., along "Embassy Row." A few small nations have embassies in New York City. Consulates are located in most large cities, and are listed in the telephone directory under "Consulates."

Conclusion

Humankind faces many challenges. Chief among these is the prevention of another world war—the development and spread of nuclear weapons threatens the existence of the human race. Other serious problems include illiteracy and starvation among many of the peoples of the world, a rapidly growing population, environmental pollution, and declining fuel reserves. Only through international cooperation can these problems successfully be met.

At the same time, communications and trade among countries will continue to increase and become more sophisticated. A Scout today could be in 15 years a businessman living in Europe, a teacher living in Africa, or a technician living in South America.

To face the challenges and opportunities of the world community both now and in the future, a Scout should, as is said in Denmark, "Vaer Beredt," or in Mexico, "Siempre Listo," or in the U.S., "Be Prepared."

Books About Citizenship

Recommended by the American Library Association's Advisory Committee to Scouting

Archer, Jules. *Hunger on Planet Earth*. Crowell, 1977.

Asimov, Isaac. *Earth: Our Crowded Spaceship*. John Day, 1974.

Blumberg, Rhoda. *Famine*. Watts, 1978.

Branley, Franklyn M. *Feast or Famine: The Energy Future*. Crowell, 1980.

Ellis, Harry B. *Ideals and Ideologies: Communism, Socialism, and Capitalism*. World, 1968.

Gregor, Arthur S. *Man's Work on the Land: The Changing Environment From the Stone Age to the Age of Smog, Sewage, and Tar on Your Feet*. Scribner, 1974.

Hoyt, Edwin P. *American Attitude: The Story of the Making of Foreign Policy in the U.S.* Abelard, 1971.

Larsen, Peter. *The United Nations at Work Throughout the World*. Lothrop, 1971.

Liston, Robert A. *The United States and the Soviet Union: A Background Book on the Struggle for Power*. Parents Magazine Press, 1973.

Madison, Arnold. *American Global Diplomacy: 1800-1950*. Watts, 1977.

Miles, Betty. *Save the Earth! An Ecology Handbook for Kids*. Knopf, 1974.

Neal, Harry E. *Communication: From Stone Age to Space Age*. Messner, 1974.

Paradis, Adrian A. *The Bulls and the Bears*. Hawthorne, 1967.

Paradis, Adrian A. *International Trade in Action*. Messner, 1973.

Pringle, Laurence P. *The Economic Growth Debate: Are There Limits to Growth?* Watts, 1978.

Pringle Laurence P. *Nuclear Power: From Physics to Politics*. Macmillan, 1979.

Pringle, Laurence P. *Our Hungry Earth: The World Food Crisis.* Macmillan, 1976.

Sechrist, Elizabeth Hough. *It's Time for Brotherhood.* Macrae, 1973.

Warner, Matt. *Your World—Your Survival!* Abelard-Schuman, 1970.

Other Sources

International Peace Academy
777 United Nations Plaza
New York, NY 10017

United Nations Sales Section
Room LX 2300
United Nations
New York, NY 10017

World Federalists Association
1424 Sixteenth Street, NW.
Washington, DC 20036

Credits

Illustrations by Joel Armstrong